HABITUDE WARRIOR'S

THE SECRET HABITUDES

QUOTES & NOTES

Develop the mind-set of a "HABITUDE WARRIOR"

by ERIK E. SWANSON

SECRET HABITUDES

"SECRET HABITUDES"
Develop the Mind-set of a
"HABITUDE WARRIOR"
by
ERIK E. SWANSON

This publication was printed in the United States of America!
Erik was made in Nicaragua, and assembled in the U.S.A.!

Published by Habitude Warrior, Inc. Erik E. Swanson

Secret Habitudes by Erik E. Swanson
Library of Congress Cataloging-in-Publication Data
ISBN: 978-0-9894136-0-2

About Erik Swanson

Erik Swanson has delivered over 3,330 motivational presentations at conferences and meetings worldwide. As a leading award winning Professional Speaker, Author & Success & Habits Coach, Erik Swanson is in great demand! Speaking on average to more than 50,000 people per year, he is both versatile in his approach and effective in facilitating a wide array of training topics.

Erik's stories hit home as he shares real life experiences which we all can relate to from his humble beginnings to where he is now. Erik shares the stage with some of the most talented speakers and trainers of the world, and now his peers, such as Brian Tracy, Jack Canfield, Les Brown, Frank Shankwitz, Greg Scott Reid, Nik Halik, Sharon Lechter, Rhonda Britten, John Assaraf, Ruben Gonzalez, Berny Dohrmann, Loral Langemeier, Scott Duffy, David Corbin, Bob Burg, Ron White, James Malinchak... and even the late, great Jim Rohn back in the day!

What they say about ERIK E. SWANSON

"Apply the HABITUDE WARRIOR Mind-set and watch your habits and relationships change rapidly. "

- Brian Tracy - Author/Speaker

"Erik is the guy I go to for my personal coaching to raise my level of success!"

- Scott Duffy - The Launch Guy/Business Strategist

"Apply Erik's teachings, wisdom and awesomeness and watch your life change."

- Ruben Gonzalez - 4 Time Olympian

"Erik teaches you how to stay on top of your game everyday! And that game is the game of life."

- Frank Shankwitz - Founder - Make a Wish Foundation

"You were YOU and you bring the awesome to the party, Erik!"

- David Corbin - Author/Speaker/Filmmaker

"Erik, you really do have the unique ability to teach the success techniques and principals needed in today's selling field and beyond. Even if you are not in sales, you connect with your audience to share ideas that are proven to assist their lives in so many ways. You have my vote !"

- Jack Canfield - Co-Author of Chicken Soup for the Soul

What they say about Erik's Presentations

"Invite Erik to speak to your group
You'll be glad you did."

- Les Brown - Speaker/Author

"Erik is one of the best speakers I have ever heard! He's funny, quick witted and just simply awesome! He will move your crowd."

- David Stanley - Filmmaker & Producer

"The Speaker Camp that Erik runs is the highest in the world in turning out 7 figure incomes! "

- Berny Dohrmann - Founder - CEO Space Int.

Motivate & Inspire Your Whole Team, Children, School, or Church Group!

The Secret Habitudes Quotes & Notes

Have you ever noticed that our attitudes can sometimes wander and we sometimes allow others to determine how we think and act. Take control of your own attitudes by developing the mind-set of a winner & the mind-set of a Habitude Warrior to develop the habit of a daily positive attitude. People will start gravitating towards you in such a positive way and you will start seeing amazing changes in your life. Don't let others decide who you are. Share these principles with your team members at work; with your kids; with the school or church group!

HABITUDE WARRIOR'S
THESECRET HABITUDES

QUOTES & NOTES

Develop the mind-set of a
"HABITUDE WARRIOR"

by ERIK E. SWANSON

Special Quantity Discounts:

$14.95 each
10-20 Books $12.95 each
21-99 Books $11.95 each
100-499 Books $10.95 each
500-999 Books $9.95 each
1001+ Books $7.95 each

SECRET HABITUDES

Turn Your Next Meeting into a 'HABITUDE' Event!

To check Erik's availability,
call 888-210-8020

BookErik@SpeakerErik.com

www.HabitudeWarrior.com

"SECRET HABITUDES TRAINING COURSE

~ **Develop the Mind-set of a HABITUDE WARRIOR"** takes you from where you are to where you want to be! Erik has designed his 'Habitude Warrior' system to take you through a year long season with him personally with 50 weekly Secret Habitude Training modules. Each week you will learn a new Habitude and will have exercises to complete to grow to the next level. Then Season Two starts right up, right away!

THE PLATINUM 48 CLUB

We also have a very special Mastermind Group called The Platinum 48! To learn more about this very exclusive group which meets in a certain cities once a month throughout the U.S. & Canada, please email us at **Platinum48@HabitudeWarrior.com**

HABITUDE WARRIOR CERTIFICATIONS

Would you like to become a Certified Habitude Warrior Trainer to teach your groups in your own city? Feel free to request info **CertifiedTrainer@HabitudeWarrior.com**

“Develop the Habit of a Great Attitude! You Deserve It!”

- Erik E. Swanson

1 The Power of Habitude Warrior Training

We are all creatures of habit! Some habits assist us in life and some hold us back from our dreams and ambitions. It's time to take control of them all. One of the absolute, best gifts you can do for yourself, and the ones your love, is give yourself the gift of the power of knowledge and the know-how to harness & utilize that knowledge. Most people in the world leave their habits and attitudes up to the world to decide instead of taking complete control of their own lives. I personally challenge you TODAY to vow to yourself to develop the Habitude Warrior Mindset & allow this system to assist you in creating great new habits as well as maintaining an awesome positive attitude throughout each and every day!

2 The Power of Setting Clear & Concise Goals

Goals are merely visions on paper with specifics attached! Only about 3% of the population actually write down their goals. That's NUTS! That means 97% do not. I'm also finding that about 97% of the population actually work for the top 3%! I wonder if there's a big correlation there. I wonder where YOU are! People are typically scared of writing their goals in fear of not accomplishing them. Don't be that person. The more specific and timely you are the more likely you are to accomplish them. Set a goal NOW to start setting goals daily. Take a blank piece of paper & write down your goals and tasks in each of these topics (one page per topic): Income, Career, Health/Fitness, Family/Relationships, & Spiritual.

3 The Power of Recalling Everyone's Names

Stop saying to yourself "Now, don't forget their name!" Start saying to yourself "You know, I'm REALLY great at recalling people's names!" People LOVE to hear their own name. It's simply getting your sub-conscious mind in-congruency with your conscious mind to be excellent at this Habitude. I used to ask people to spell their name again when I had forgotten it... they would say "B-O-B, how do you spell BOB?"

Use these 3 steps I call "Bracketing." It helps tremendously. My record now is recalling 158 names in one meeting.

1. Place their name at the beginning of your first sentence
2. Place their name at the end of your next sentence
3. Repeat their name 3 to 5 times. **NOT OUT LOUD !!!**

4 The Power of Creating Great New Habits

Creating habits is a habit... meaning it takes a system to develop a habit in changing your existing ones. The rule of thumb is that a habit CAN'T be broken, it can merely be replaced. So, the trick is to replace your existing bad habits with ones that are much better & direct your life in a positive motion towards your ultimate goal. First, you need to take an inventory of your limiting habits that are unhealthy or holding you back in areas of your life. Identifying them is critical. Next, write a list of pro's and con's attached to having that bad habit and having a much healthier habit to replace it with. Next, *(and, THIS IS HUGE!)* write down the # of years you feel this new habit will bring you in happiness and fulfillment! Now start saying to yourself & out loud, in the present tense, all day long, that you exhibit this new habit. Own it and it will now be yours! Own it and it will own you!

5 The Power of Maximizing Procrastination

Look, everyone procrastinates! And those who say they don't are just the ones who are delaying in answering the question... and they want to talk about it later.
There are 3 tricks to maximizing procrastination.

1) The first trick is to realize EVERYTHING can't get done. You will need to prioritize each task within each goal.
2) The second trick to knowing my definition of 'stress' is when you don't reach certain goals in the amount of time you've allotted yourself. Need to re-allocate the time.
3) The third trick is to be an expert in YOUR field, not in everyone else's. It's okay to ask for assistance in getting your ultimate goal accomplished. Use their time to maximize yours!

6 The Power of Communicating & Connecting

Clear & effective communication is absolutely essential to connect with others. How many times do we hear “Honey I just want you to listen to me!” Here are a few tips I remind myself daily:

1) Listen, Listen, Listen! Make sure you listen, not only with your ears, but also with your eyes and of course your brain.
2) Re-phrase their question or statement and recite it back to them in order to be very clear in what they are communicating
3) Compliment them on their thoughts and thank them for bringing it to your attention. Their thoughts are very important.

“What’s going on in the inside
always shows up on the outside.”
- Earl Nightingale -

7 The Power of Master Mind Groups

Benjamin Franklin, Napoleon Hill, Donald Trump , Brian Tracy, even the President and every highly successful person in the world all use the power of a master mind group! These groups allow you to bring topics of super importance to the table with like-minded people, but from a different vantage point. The fantastic thing about these groups is that 3 minds are better than 1... in fact, even 8 minds are better than 1. They are easy to find *if* you are actually looking for them. I always suggest to start your own group as well. This gives you more control to steer it in the direction and focus you intend. Important Note: remind yourself that you don't know it all. Absorb information and ideas from your group to broaden your personal scope and build a trust and alliance with your members. You will soon see how valuable these groups really are. Build them and they will come! To request a list of groups in your area send us an email: **mastermindgroups@habitudewarrior.com**

8 The Power of Networking & Referrals

NETWORKING

They say you are the culmination of the books you read and the people you surround yourself with. They also say 50% of the people responsible for your success you haven't even met yet! And the other 50% you already know, but haven't networked the proper way with. Zig Ziglar says "You can get everything in life you want, if you'll just help others get everything they want!" That's a *huge* concept!
Most people totally miss that very important concept and theory.
Here are my 5 Golden Rules of Networking Meeting Conduct:

1) Always bring enough business cards & bring a giveaway
2) Dress for Success. Look like you are in the top of your industry
3) Don't be Shy. Meet everyone and recall everyone's names
4) Be Early & Late! Get there early and leave late. Most things happen before and after the actual meeting. Use that time!
5) Always ask to help others instead of asking how they can help you!

REFERRALS

Referrals are so vitally important to success these days for the main fact that it's not only *what* you know, but *who* you know. Or better yet, *who knows you!*

Main reason we don't ask for referrals: FEAR!
Main reason we don't get referrals: We don't ask!
Main reason we don't get good referrals: We don't ask properly!

Here are my 5 tips on asking and getting referrals daily:

1) Write a list of 30 reasons why people should refer you and your business to others they know, like, and trust
2) Assure to yourself daily that *YOU & YOUR COMPANY* are worth people referring their closest friends, family, and clients
3) Write a detailed description of your perfect referral
4) Write a goal of how many referrals you will gather each month
5) Hire an AP (Accountability Partner) to hold you to the fire

Request information on AP's by emailing us:
AccountabilityPartners@HabitudeWarrior.com

"Who else do you know that are progressive thinkers like yourself, that you *really* trust and feel would be a good fit for what we are offering?"

9 The Power of Positive Affirmations

I USED TO HATE AFFIRMATIONS!

Guess what... I used to think ‘affirmations’ were so corny. I used to say these things never work! And guess what, they didn’t! Then I realized I was using ‘affirmations’ against myself. Now, I pump myself up EVERY DAY (just like a bicycle tire). You have to! If you’re not going to, who else will ?

My definition: *Positive Affirmations are positive statements that describe a desired outcome in which you repeat to yourself systematically throughout the day and night to program your sub-conscious mind to be in congruency with your conscious mind by triggering you into a positive action towards your goal.”*

I am the Best! Things are Awesome !
It’s going to be a Great Day!
(guess what... it usually is!)

10 The Power of Persistence

Persistence is the act of never, ever, ever, ever giving up! Believe you can do the task at hand and persist until it is accomplished. That is Habitude you want to possess at all times throughout your life. This one Habitude will change your life... because here's a little secret: most people give up! In fact, they try once; maybe twice; three times a charm... then guess what... poof, they are done. Well, just by mere 'persistence' you can outwit your competition in any area of your life. Studies have told us for many years now that about 80% of all sales and commitments are closed after about the 5th or 6th try of asking. If that's the case, just persisting will bring you over that curve and give you success beyond belief. That 'extra mile' is not traveled much.

VOW TO YOURSELF TO ALWAYS TRAVEL THAT EXTRA MILE FROM TODAY ONWARDS!

11 The Power of Rewards & Awards

Rewarding oneself if so vital to the 'success game' in that it lends a motivational component that typically leads to the positive result of any goal being sought after. Many studies have taught us that just the mere fact of having the emotional result and outcome linked to the end of a goal or task, assists us in directing our attention to that particular goal or task. And that's what you want! You want to make it as easy as possible for your brain to direct attention on to the pleasure of completing that particular task so it can assist us in every measure of sticking to the task at hand. Rewards need to be relevant, timely, realistic and directly linked to goals and tasks.

Awards are a fantastic was to motivate your team or family! The 'Did It Awesome' award is one of our favorites. In my company, we also award a different employee with their own day! Literally their own day! It's AWESOME ! Try it.

12 The Power of Law of Attraction

As I was about to write my thoughts on the Law of Attraction, a flight attendant just said to me, as she was looking over my shoulder (apparently reading my computer screen as I'm writing) "WOW, I'm reading The Secret right now!"... as she had it tucked under her arm while walking down the isle. Weird, huh? But, I have a choice to look at that as a 'coincidence' or rather a reminder of the 'law of attraction' in which I believe if you combine the old principle of 'cause and effect' with the power of thoughts, then you come up with a very powerful explanation of the 'Law of Attraction.' What you think about expands. And the simple, but powerful and useful Habitude of directing your thoughts to what you would like to see show up in your life actually lends to a higher percentage of just that happening. **So, GO FOR IT!** What would you like to show up in your life. Try it and watch it manifest ! You have everything to gain! Notice I could have said that last statement a different way, but chose to use the positive 'law of attraction' way!

13 The Power of The 1% Formula

Developing your own 1% Formula is powerful to so many areas of your life. It simply states for you to pick 5 areas in your life to improve on for that year and vow to better yourself in each area just 1% per day for 365 days a year. Most people think you will be 365% better, but in fact you will be using what's called the 'compound effect' and bettering yourself tremendously more. Then add on the fact that each of the five areas actually assists the other four.

"The man who will use his skill and constructive imagination
to see how much he can give for a dollar,
instead of how little he can give for a dollar,
is bound to succeed."
- Henry Ford -

14 The Power of Visualization

Visualization means to literally 'see' it in your mind before actually seeing it in reality. But the cool thing is that you can manifest it in your mind whichever way you would like to have it show up. So, it's your choice! Be bold. Be awesome. Be super positive and visualize your future the way you would like it to be. Studies upon studies tell us this truly works. You are more drawn to the outcome you truly want and truly think about all day long, almost like a magnet. I like to take it steps further and teach my coaching clients (are you one of my clients yet???) to use ALL 5 senses in your visualization techniques. How does it look, feel, taste, smell, and sound when you win that trophy or accomplish that feat of success?

"If you paint in your mind a picture of bright and happy expectations, you put yourself into a condition conducive to your goal.."
- Norman Vincent Peale -

15 The Power of Voice Inflections

You have a voice... use it wisely! And the power comes within the volume and pitch and level of your voice, not just the actual words. My father used to say to me as a child 'Don't look at me in that tone of voice.' I always thought that was so funny, but now I realize it's true. You really can 'communicate' with different levels of your voice to make the impact you desire. Try matching your voice levels, pitch and spacing of your words with someone you are speaking with and watch them respond in a more favorable way towards you without even noticing. Now remember, only use this technique for good, not for evil!

"Knowledge speaks, wisdom listens, and the heart knows!"
- Erik Swanson -

16 The Power of Self Improvement

To improve oneself is probably the single most important strategy of success to accomplish in your life. The funny thing is, once you start you can never finish! Think about it. The very act of this Habitude is to constantly improve and the realization that there is always room for improvement. Hey, what's the biggest room in the world, ROOM FOR IMPROVEMENT! I just made that up! Ha ha, I know I'm a riot. Philosopher Jim Rohn used to tell us to work harder on yourself than your job or careers and not only will your careers flourish, but your whole life will flourish right in front of you. There is a Japanese term called Kaizen which simply means the act of constantly improving. Then our friend Tony Robbins coined the term CANI which simply means Constant And Never-ending Improvement. I implement this Habitude with the 1% Formula and life starts to rock!

17 The Power of Mentoring

Mentoring is a perfect way for you to practice your craft while teaching it at the same time. Whether you know it or not, everyone is a mentor to someone. Most people don't realize it. Children are always looking at adult's actions and emulating them. Monkey see - monkey do. So, watch out for those who are following in your steps. Becoming a true mentor to someone (or many people) is an amazing and very satisfying feeling. The very act of helping and guiding others to success is extremely noble. You can start by mentoring a niece or nephew. Mentor at your church group. Then learn to become a Coach. We actually train coaches to become mentors in what we call 'Coach the Coach.' Mentoring also strengthens your Habitude of constantly improving and searching out new and exciting tips and techniques to success in your field. Become a mentor! You'll love it!

18 The Power of Journaling

Write it down! Do it daily. Take my advice right here and now. It was one of the best pieces of advice handed down to me by one of my mentors and good friend, Mary Ellen Davis. She explained to me "Erik, you have a story, tell it. You have a voice, share it. You have a life, make it memorable." She explained to me that if I journaled each and every day, by the end of a year I would have a book in me and I simply needed to get it to the publishers. She was right! And I thank her immensely for it. Journaling needs to be a daily Habitude. It gets much easier each day you do it. And when you reflect back for the year, you will have a beautiful story filled with love, triumphs, some heart-ache, amazing feats of success, and so much more.

"I never did a day's work in my life.
It was all fun."
- Thomas Edison -

19 The Power of Testimonials

They say it's not what you know; but, who you know. I like to say: it's who knows you! I also like to remind myself: it's what people know you are saying about you that matters tremendously. I learned very early on and it's developed into a Habitude, that testimonials are worth a thousand words. The best way to get a testimony from someone is by these words below:

"How can I get that in writing? Or better yet, let's do a quick 30 second video with you introducing yourself and your services and then giving me a great testimony so that it's a win-win for both of us!"

I have tremendous results by using that simple phrase above. The #1 reason why people don't get testimonials is simply because they never asked for them. Start asking for them daily ! Can you challenge yourself to get 1 per week for the next 52 weeks?

20 The Power of Passing It On

My great friend, Speaker, Author and a Filmmaker, Greg S. Reid, produced a movie with the same name of "PASS IT ON." The whole premise of this Habitude is two fold:

1) Don't die with your song inside of you! Pass it on to others so they can learn and grow from your experience, knowledge and wisdom.

2) Help others by passing on your good fortunes and assist the world in being a better place. Similar to 'paying it forward,' passing it on to others without any hesitation, ego, or recognition is key.

"Give a man a fish and he will eat for a day.
Teach a man to fish and he will eat for the rest of his life."
- Chinese Proverb -

21 The Power of Quantum Physics

Wow, Quantum Physics! Ugh, I have no idea about this subject. Or do I? I've learned that everything has a molecular makeup that are super small and vibrate at different frequencies. Friends and teachers such as John Assaraf from the Secret and Sharon Lechter from Out Witting The Devil, explain to us that there is not much difference between a Porsche and a Possum. Really the only difference is how fast the vibrations are moving. Matter is matter. I agree. Wow, what a theory. Can you use that in your personal life? Can you 'wake up' your matter and make it move at a faster speed and vibration? Can you slow it down when needed to conserve energy and connect with people more on 'that speed'? See what I mean? Mind you, it's a theory, but it's also a 'thought' and well, by definition, all 'thoughts' have speed and vibration! Your Habitude assignment right now is to think about your thoughts. And think in which ways can you direct your thoughts to get your conscious mind and your sub-conscious mind in congruency with one-another. Good luck, and GO!

22 The Power of a Positive Attitude

You have a choice! It's completely up to you. Either way, occurrences are going to happen. It's totally up to you to choose the way you think throughout each and every day. Stop allowing other people to rent space in your mind. If you systematically remind yourself each day and in front of every challenge to ask yourself this question: "How would a positive leader think and feel in the midst of this experience?"... and then act and emulate this way. It sounds simple, doesn't it. Guess what, IT IS! It's that simple. They say 'common sense' isn't that common. Maintaining a positive attitude in my life has changed my life in so many ways. People now call me 'The Energy Guy' or 'The guy who brings the Awesome!' I love that and wouldn't change it for the world. In fact, because I'm so positive, it literally rubs off on others throughout the day and makes the world spin just a bit nicer each day. Be someone's Awesomeness! But, remember, it starts within.

23 The Power of Daily Learning

People in many other countries would walk miles upon miles to just get the chance to attend a school to learn. They are eager and willing to learn. Suggestion: never stop learning. Use your gift of learning power and make it into a Habitude. I constantly tell people 'I'm still in school!' Put it this way, If the world is spinning on it's axis 365 days a year, and you stay stagnant in not learning or applying, then, are you really staying stagnant OR are you actually moving ***backwards***? Seek out the experts in each field you choose to grow in. The five major categories are: Career, Income, Spiritual, Health/Fitness, and Family/Relationships. Vow to apply the 1% formula and learn each day from a new expert per month.

"He who undertakes to be his own teacher
has a fool for a pupil."

- Chinese Proverb -

24 The Power of Social Media Networking

Let's face it, social media is here to stay and is what I call 'The New Normal.' And let's also face it, I think the internet is going to stick around as well. So, you have 2 choices: Either constantly complain OR confidently conquer! I choose to conquer. One of the best Habitudes I've developed for my business is to commit to introducing myself to at least 7 new social media contacts per day. But, you must do it in a natural and organic way... meaning write a nice quick personal note to these 7 new contacts per day. Get to know them. Find out how you can help them. Zig Ziglar used to tell us that the more you help others get what they want, the more you end up getting what you want. Join as many like minded social media groups you can find that will assist you in aligning yourself with the right type of contacts.

"You gain strength, courage, and confidence every time you look fear in the face."

- Eleanor Roosevelt -

25 The Power of Closing Techniques

The best closing techniques are obviously the ones that don't even seem like they are closing techniques. Do you know the #1 reason why people don't get 'the close?' It's because we never asked for the 'close!' Tons of studies tell us that the prospect would have bought, had the sales professional simply asked the prospect to buy. But, we simply don't ask. Why don't we ask: Fear! Here's a tip: Always act as if you are confident and not afraid of asking for the close. Also, use what I call the 30 list. The 30 List is simply a list of 30 reasons why you feel the prospect should take advantage of your product or service. Make a list and keep adding to this 30 list. Convince yourself before you convince others. There are so many closing techniques I could share with you. Here's one:

*'We are not trying to be the low **cost** provider. We are the low **risk** provider.' (this implies that others are cutting their costs and you get what you pay for, right) 'We are the low RISK provider... no one wants to take a big risk, especially in this investment in you and your family!'*

26 The Power of Objection Handling

Objection Handling is just the name of the game. And it's part of the game. You absolutely need to get GREAT at it! It's where a ton of sales people lose the deal and I'm here to help you with it right now. Here's 5 steps to handling an objection of any kind:

1) Acknowledge them and their objection and compliment them.
   (*Actually compliment them for bringing it up to your attention)*
2) Pause and Use their Name
   (*Using their name and pausing makes them feel more comfortable)*
3) Rephrase and Question the Objection
   (*Literally recite the question back to them by rephrasing it)*
4) S-H-U-T-U-P
   (*Actually be super quiet here and allow them to speak)*
5) Answer It
   (*Give them a concise and accurate answer explaining how and why the value of the product or service far outweighs the price)*

27 The Power of Single Handling

This technique is an amazing way to keep your time management in line. People tend to focus on many things at once (I call it 'majoring in minor things') when in reality simply focusing on one task at hand and finishing it to completion saves you a tremendous amount of ramp up and getting started time. It is said that a full 80% of your success will be derived by 20 % of the things you focus in on. Even with that study, people tend to focus on the other 80% of non-productive items that lead to mediocrity.

"Until we can manage time,
we can manage nothing else."

- Peter Drucker -

28 The Power of High Fiving Perfect Strangers

One of my favorite Habitudes is to high five 5 perfect strangers by noon each day! It's AWESOME! Why do I do it? Well, when I was learning the art of selling I found out that all selling really is, is a transfer of enthusiasm. If I can transfer my great attitude to others in this world, then sign me up! The trick is that you must have a great attitude in advance. Now, what's really cool is that when you high five someone you don't know when you're walking by them in the street or parking lot or in a coffee shop (I do this everywhere, except for NYC!) you'll notice they will innately have an instant smile on their face and a bounce in their step. And of course I hope it carries on to the next person once they high five someone they don't know. It's contagious in the best possible way. Set a goal today to high five 5 strangers by noon each and every day. Oh, by noon you may wonder. Well, if you're in sales or an entrepreneur, then you know you must get **out of the house** and meet prospects!

29 The Power of Behavioral Contracting

Behavioral Contracting is the act of committing and communicating with your relationships in such a fashion to be clear with each party in what you (and they) expect out of the relationship. Being crystal clear up front is one of the most important facets of any relationship, whether personal or business. I owe this technique to my Mother who taught me the wisdom of clarity in advance. She always used to tell me to be very clear in what I want out of the relationship as it will help you in the long run. She is extremely wise, and beautiful of course!

Behavioral Contract with yourself as well in your actions and behaviors. Try to 21 day challenge in contracting with yourself to not complain for 21 days straight. Yup, it's tough... at first. Then it gets much easier.

"Satisfaction lies in the effort, not in the attainment.
Full effort is full victory."
- Gandhi -

30

The Power of Staying Calm, Cool & Collective

This is a technique I learned by one of my close friends, Speaker, Author, and 4 Time Olympian, Ruben Gonzalez! He taught me that athletes have a system to deal with stress and all athletes use this system. One aspect of this system I decided to implement in my own business and personal life as well. Meditation and Yoga also implement this system. Even the book ***The Secret*** refers to it's ability to get the result you desire. When confronted with any adversity simply recite these words to yourself over and over again:

'Stay Calm. Stay Cool. Stay Collective. Stay Calm, Stay Cool. Stay Collective. Stay Calm. Stay Cool. Stay Collective.'

Just the act of saying these words to yourself and believing them will enhance your ability to do exactly what the words imply. Check him out at www.OlympicMotivation.com & tell him I sent ya!

31 The Power of the Unconscious Mind

There is a Habitude technique sometimes referred to as 'The 4 Stages of Utopia.' It refers to bringing your skill level from the 'Unconscious Incompetent' to the 'Unconscious Competent.' The Power of the Unconscious Mind is the act of getting your unconscious mind in congruency with your conscious mind, and visa-versa. This is a purposeful task and must be treated like that at all times.

The technique is as such:

1) take 5 to 10 min at the end of the day when you are just ready to fall asleep and focus and visualize on your goals at hand. This is also called 'TOMA' which stands for Top Of Mind Awareness.
2) take 5 to 10 min at the beginning of your day when you just wake up to reflect, focus and visualize your day at hand keeping it in congruency with your goals at hand.

32 The Power of Humor & Personality

BE FUNNY !!!

People love it. I can't tell you how many times people respond to me in such a positive way when I poke fun of myself and use my humor in my daily personality. Times are too tough to take things seriously every single second of the day. If you speak to groups or even on an appointment, I break the ice with a quick witted funny saying. Notice I didn't say to open or break the ice with a 'joke.' You always run a risk of someone not really liking the joke and you will start off in the negative at that point. I remember when I was in college and wanted to get a date, I constantly heard that all the girls loved a guy with a great sense of humor. So, be Chandler from the T.V. show Friends if you have to. But, BE FUNNY! When you make the other person laugh it sends a message to their unconscious part of their brain allowing them to relax and feel good about the situation. Hey, suggestion: **BE FUNNY!**

"Be yourself; everyone else is already taken."
- Oscar Wilde -

33 The Power of the “WIN” Concept

The “WIN” Concept is a way of life for me. I learned early on that the way to get anything you want in life, you have to be able and willing to help others get whatever they want in life. At the bottom of one of my close friend’s emails is the sentence: How may I be of service? And guess, what, he means it. It’s simple, help others get what they want, and by the law of attraction and what goes around comes around, you will soon get what you were looking for too. Oh and It doesn’t hurt having everyone in congruency to assist you because he were so gracious in assisting them. Make sense ? I take it one step further and use my “Plus One Theory” by doing just one or two extra things that people weren’t expecting in order to go that extra mile for them. We also call it ‘Guerrilla Kindness” where you do nice things for people all the time, but you don’t look or expect any recognition. The “WIN” Concept will take your life to new levels!

34 The Power of Giving Back

A great friend of mine named Frank started a really cool association! He was sitting around his house in Arizona with his wife Kitty, focusing on some of their stuff (you know, bills, etc) when a knock on their door came and an opportunity was presented in their lives to assist someone very special. You see, their neighbor's son, little Christian, was diagnosed with Leukemia at age 6. One of Christian's 'wishes' was to be a sheriff of a town. Well you probably guessed it as to who my good friend is. Right then and there Frank Shankwitz founded a small little organization called '*Make a Wish Foundation*'! He gave back! What kind of opportunities do you have in front of you that you have overlooked or passed by to really make a difference and give back. We all leave this world. How will you leave it? How will you be remembered for your contributions to this beautiful world. Here's a suggestion: stop complaining! I use a technique called "TWC" which simply reminds me that 40 % of our world's population live in 'third world countries' who don't even have the luxuries we all do. Give back now!

35 The Power of the Abundance Theory

Do me a favor and reach into your pocket right now and pull out a crisp hundred dollar bill. Did you do it. Can you do it? If you can't do that, then you're not living by the Abundance Theory. There's actually a secret society of people around the world who know this little action of this technique. And, well, now you do. In fact, we trade the bills between each other as to metaphorically 'spread the wealth.' It's a 'mind-set' in which someone should always be able to ask you for a hundred dollar bill, and you always have one or two, or five on you. Try it. You start shifting your mind-set in the way of abundance. You start seeing things differently. You start seeing that you **CAN** afford anything you set your mind to... instead of focusing on the things you **CAN'T** afford. Make sense. Can you think of other areas in your life you can apply this theory to? Make a list in the 5 major areas of your life and see where your mind-set may be getting in your own way.

36 The Power of Friend Renewal Contracting

We all have friends. But, are they true friends? I teach this technique of Friend Renewal Contracting in order for you to free up more time in your life to actually meet the right people who should really be there. Let's face it, life and friends take up time. Are you spending that time wisely with those who are truly friends who are contributing to the betterment of you and others. It may seem harsh, but each year I suggest decide who you would like to renew their 'friend card' with for the next year. Yup, that's right... I look at each of my relationships (friends and business) and determine whether it's worth renewing another year. Are they contributing to the positive enhancement of the relationship or are they acting like a reverse bank account in only taking withdrawals all the time instead of making valuable deposits into the relationship. You soon see who are time-wasters in your life. Here's a lesson: Stop chasing people who you are trying to give praise, money or awards. Honor yourself! You deserve it!

37 The Power of Identifying People's Needs

Once you figure out what others need, and you can assist them in getting what they truly want, then you start getting what **you** truly want as well. Here is an acronym we use to identify people's needs:

N: NOW - Where are they 'now? Find out where they are coming from so you can move them to where they would like to go.
E: ENJOY - What is it that the 'enjoy' about where they are now?
E: ENVIRONMENT - What is the environment they are seeking?
D: DECISIONS - Who was in the decision making process?
S: SOLUTIONS - Ultimately offer your solution to assist them!

The problem with most people is they simply don't find out what the client's past was and why they chose that past, and who chose that past for them. Identify these items and now you have the foundation to move them to the ultimate solution: YOU and YOUR services!

38 The Power of Presentation Skills

This is so vital to any talk, speech, appointment, conversation, and life! Schools should make this Habitude a must for every student.

Here is a 7 key checklist you must have:

1) Know your material! Knowledge of your material is key to not have to worry about fumbling in your speech.
2) Know your audience! Who are you speaking to. What is the focus of the talk? What is the message your audience is seeking?
3) Know your timing! Don't run over. Run a few minutes short... everyone will thank you for doing so. Trust me!
4) PROJECT your voice. If people can't hear you, people won't listen!
5) Get the audience to participate. Ask questions you already know the audience knows the answers to.
6) Quote great leaders of the world and sprinkle them in.
7) Have fun! Be Funny! Make fun of yourself in a good way!

39 The Power of Public Speaking

Get on stage!

It's one of the best things you can do for your business and even for your personal life. When you step on stage you automatically elevate yourself as an expert in your field. It puts you in the light of greatness and if you can align yourself to share the stages with other great speakers, authors, leaders, all the better. In fact, I personally built, founded and am the CEO of a seminar company for the specific reason of aligning myself to share the stage with my mentors and other amazing speakers. You don't have to be a speaker to use the Power of Public Speaking. You are an expert in your specific field of work or abilities. Develop what is called a 'keynote speech' of about 30 to 40 minutes in length, in what it takes to make it or break it in your business. Here, I'll even give you your title of your talk. You ready?

"The 7 Strategies You Absolutely Need To Know In ...."

or

"The Awesome Tips Of An Unlikely Entrepreneur"

40 The Power of the 60 Second Morning Mirror

Take 60 seconds every morning when you get up and walk over to your mirror in the bathroom. Stare right into your own eyes and say these words:

I'm the best, I'm the best, I'm the best, I'm the best, I'm the best, I'm the best, I'm the best, I'm the best, I'm the best, I'm the best, I'm the best, I'm the best, I'm the best, I'm the best, I AM THE BEST !!!!

After about the tenth or twelfth time in saying it, you actually start believing it. You need to pump yourself up in the morning (every morning) to make it an awesome day. I even write it on my mirror so I see it every morning. Who else better to pump yourself up than **YOU! YOU REALLY ARE THE BEST!**

41

The Power of Healthy Eating & Drinking

They say you are what you eat. Guess what, you really are. We learn through many studies that there's a direct correlation between eating healthy and productivity. I now choose what I put in to my body. Wanna lose 10 lbs quick (or like I did when I lost 24 lbs in a course of a 14 week period). Cool, this is what I did... here's my plan:

- Reach for bottled water instead of coffee, teas or sodas
- Reach for grilled chicken or grilled fish (salmon rocks!)
- Reach for grilled asparagus and grilled squash and zucchini
- Reach for non-fat greek yogurt if you want a treat
- Reach for blueberries, strawberries, and bananas

Simply cut out the starches and carbs and bread, etc. The feeling of a little hunger in your belly is cool. Remember use the 'TWC" Theory.

42 The Power of Healthy Exercising

There are studies that link health exercising with a long life of prosperity. The tip is to start small and grow... .meaning don't try and run a marathon your first day you decide to exercise. Baby steps is key. But, another key to remember is to do one thing every day a little bit more that leads you to your ultimate goal. So, start by walking a few blocks a day for a week. Then, move it up to a mile every other day for a couple weeks. It starts becoming a habit. That's what you want! Dr. Wayne Dyer swims a few miles a day and hasn't taken a break from that Habitude in about 40 or 50 years! It's a habit he will never leave or break. That's AWESOME! Start now! You deserve it.

"What happens to you is less significant than
what happens within you."

- Louis Mann -

43

The Power of The Cycle of Achievement

The Cycle of Achievement is a Habitude I developed to remind me to not focus on just one aspect of my life, but to have a focused balance in all 4 major areas of my life. Here they are:

Financial - Faith - Family - Fitness

Now, I'm not sure about you... but have you noticed that sometimes when you're working so diligently on let's say your financial goals (income and career), you may be lacking in building and growing some of the other 3 areas such as family or fitness? You need to keep a balance. I literally have a check list to make sure I'm devoting time and energy and excitement and enthusiasm and awesomeness in each of the areas to keep a beautiful balance. As my good friend, James Malinchak, likes to always refer to the fact that you need all four legs of a chair to hold that foundation of the chair up.

44 The Power of 'San Diego'

Wow, I can't believe I'm giving you this Habitude! This is a Secret Habitude I only share with my personal coaching clients when we are one- on-one. But, hey, It's a bonus for you now. Let me ask you a question. Where are you right now? Where do you want to be right now? Why aren't you there?!!! Simple answer is because you did not make a decision to be there. You may have thought about it. You may even had talked about it. You may even had it written down as a goal of yours. BUT, you're still not there. WHY! Reason... you haven't acted upon it. Here's a tip. **DO IT**! For me, I always wanted to live in sunny San Diego. But, I always had a reason why to push it off to another year or say 'someday, when...' My friend Greg Reid calls it the 'Once Eyes" which really stands for 'once I do this or that, then I'll do it.' Again, my tip: **DO IT NOW**! That old saying 'Build it and they will come" is so true. Trust me, you'll figure out a way to sustain it. The hardest part is just getting off your 'assets' and doing it. So, for me, it was San Diego! What's yours? PS: I have so many coaching clients thanking me for this one tip that changed their life forever. Send me your stories!

45

The Power of Reading

Charlie Tremendous Jones once said that you are the culmination of the books you read and the people you surround yourself with. I truly believe that. Which books have you read or have you not read yet that would have a tremendous amount of impact in your life right now? Here's what I do. I buy 3 copies of the same exact book. I keep one at my home in my study, I keep another copy next to my bed, and I keep a third copy in one of my cars. I pull out the copy in my car whenever I can and read a chapter here and there. Even at a traffic light. Trust me people will tell you when it's time to put the book down and get moving. Then I seek out the author and have him sign one of my books and I keep that in my study forever. You should see the collection I now have. And if those 2 above ideas weren't already priceless... check this third one: I take the 3rd book and I donate it to a child in need... to someone who can learn from it and grow. Be someone's mentor and change the world to be an AWESOME PLACE!

46 The Power of Being a 'Loser'

BEING A LOSER? Yeah, be a loser! I learned this from my buddy Ruben Gonzalez who was once asked what he did for a living... He said he was a "luger." Which, right away they replied "don't call yourself that!" They didn't realize he was referring to the winter olympic sport called the Luge. So, it got me thinking. One of my new Habitudes is to train yourself to become a 'loser' in that you **lose** the bad attitude if you have one. You lose the ego if you bring that to the table one day. You lose that procrastination gland that so many of us have in our lives. What is something YOU CAN LOSE in your life that will open up so much more opportunities and doors of your dreams and goals. You know, it's not always a 'to do' list we need to have, but a 'NOT to do' list that truly makes a difference. Implement this Habitude and become a WINNER!

"Your attitude is too precious to hurt by second-guessing yourself. Protect your attitude because it's the key to your future success"

- Ruben Gonzalez -

47 The Power of Stories & Experiences

People love stories and you can draw your stories from your experiences all the time. A polished speaker, author, trainer, coach, mom, dad, friend, knows that the art of getting your point across to others lies within how well you can capture and keep their attention. Implement this Habitude and watch people tend to gravitate towards you like they've never done before. Draw off of your experiences that are kinda funny to look back and reflect on. I have made it a habit to exchange stories with my friends and my significant other and ask them really pondering questions about their childhood so that I can draw cool ideas off of them that trigger my memory of my childhood and things I can draw off of. Make sense? They don't even know that I'm doing it. Oops, well, if they read this then they'll know where some of my latest stories were inspired by. Hey, hats off to them for allowing me to learn from them, right?!

48 The Power of Nicknames

What's your nickname? Do you have one? Get one! All Superhero's have one. Aren't you a Superhero? Ask 20 of your friends what they would call you if you had one. I've had many nicknames over the years that suited me during those times. One of my first was given to me by my friends back in Texas. They called me "Styles" because I always seemed to have my own style of doing things which made me fun to be around, they said. Then it changed to "Mr. Brightside" as I always looked for the bright side of things and rarely complain, but instead sought out the positive message or teachings even during adversity. Then it went to "Mr. AWESOME" which of course I still am! And now, I'm called:

"Mr. HABITUDES!"

Nicknames makes your memorable... and that's what you want!
You want to stand out in a crowd. **Be a SUPERHERO!**

49 The Power of the 8 Minute Rule

I thank my beautiful girlfriend, best friend, and life mentor, Dalila, for this Habitude. You ever get in an argument with someone close to you and all you want to do is keep arguing until they agree with you. Well, I guess I was doing that one day and I noticed that Dali had stopped arguing back and she was just super quiet. So, I thought I had 'won' and I stopped arguing as well. Well, it lasted about 8 minutes... until, I finally broke the silence and we started talking about a totally different subject. We were back to our loving selves again. I soon realized that she used the 8 minute rule in just walking away from the disagreement for a full 8 minutes and this would refresh her loving and caring attitude as she reminded herself why she cares for me in the first place. We soon forgot why we were even arguing in the first place. Sometimes all you need is a little bit of time to regroup yourself. Great Habitude! Thank you ***Baby*!**

"If the only tool you have is a hammer,
you tend to see every problem as a nail."
- Abraham Harold Maslow -

50 The Power of Being a Better Person

A good friend, Speaker, Author and colleague of mine, Doug Grady, once told me that there was a study done a few years ago in finding America's top 10 new year's resolutions for that year. I was curious what was on it. Aren't you? Well, let's guess. Yup, I'm sure you guessed some of them right off the bat: lose weight, stop smoking, eat healthier, exercise more, make more money, get a better job, etc. Guess what was on the bottom of the list (but still made the top 10)... "Be a Better Person!" Wow, can you believe it? It was at the bottom of this top 10 list. Wouldn't you agree that if you stick that right at the very top of the list and make it #1, then all of the other 9 would be super easy to accomplish? Be a better person. That's my motto. What area of your life can you improve to help others and help you at the very same time? Make a list of 30 things you can do this week to direct yourself to a "Better Person Living!" Do it and watch your life grow to it's fullest potential.

The Habitude Warrior's Creed

SWANSON'S CREED !

I am the best
I am focused
I will succeed
I believe in myself
I have the will to win
I set high expectations
I visualize my perfect future
I don't let others bring me down
I surround myself with winners
I will learn and grow everyday !

Free Gifts from Erik

To sign up for Erik's Monthly Success Tips
and to watch Erik's video filled
with tips you can use to succeed more in life:

Visit:

www.HabitudeWarrior.com

To book Erik for your next meeting,
conference or event call
888-210-8020

SECRET HABITUDES